MW01269097

"*Scorn not the sonnet ... with this key Shakespeare unlocked his heart.*"
– William Wordsworth

"*He breathed upon dead bodies and brought them into life.*"
– Ralph Waldo Emerson

AN ACT OF WILL

or

The Secret Life of William Shakespeare

by

Michael McEvoy

First performed at The Third International Theatre Festival, Lahore, Pakistan 12th November 1999.

49Knights
Independent Publishing House
Edinburgh & Cambridge

Text © 2019 by Michael McEvoy
Typeset © 2019 by 49Knights

Rights of performance by amateurs are controlled by the author, Michael McEvoy, and he, or his authorised agents, issue licences to amateurs on payment of a fee. It is an infringement of the Copyright to give any performance or public reading of this play before the fee has been paid and the license issued.

The Royalty Fee is subject to contract, and subject to variation, at the sole discretion of the author, Michael McEvoy.

The basic fee for each and every performance by amateurs is available upon request from admin@writersguild.org.uk.

The Professional Rights in this playscript are controlled by the author, Michael McEvoy, who bears sole responsibility should there be found within any infringement upon the personal rights of any third party, including, without limitation, claims in defamation, privacy, copyright, or trademark.

The publication of this play does not imply that it is necessarily available for performance by amateurs or professionals, either in the British Isles or Overseas. Amateurs and professionals considering a production are strongly advised, in their own interests, to apply to the appropriate agents for consent prior to starting rehearsals or booking a venue.

The fact that a play is published by 49Knights, Independent Publishing House, Edinburgh & Cambridge, does not indicate that performance rights are available, or that 49Knights controls such rights.

ISBN: 978-1-9993658-3-7

Please see page 6 for further copyright information.

An Act of Will: The Secret Life of William Shakespeare

An Act of Will by Michael McEvoy

Forewords by Steven Canny & Ken Pickering

Text edited by Dan Lentell

Cover design by Nicky Browne

Incidental artwork by Simon Bramble

Original portrait of the author by Imogen Wilde

Typesetting by Sean Baker

Further information about plays, licensing can be requested from
admin@writersguild.org.uk

COPYRIGHT INFORMATION

(See also page 4)

This play is fully protected under the Copyright Laws of the British Commonwealth of Nations, the United States of America and all countries of the Berne and Universal Copyright Conventions.

All rights including Stage, Motion Picture, Radio, Television, Public Reading, and Translation into Foreign Languages, are strictly reserved.

No part of this publication may be lawfully reproduced in ANY form or by any means – photocopying, typescript, recording (including video-recording), manuscript, electronic, mechanical or otherwise – or be transmitted or stored in a retrieval system, without prior permission.

Licences for amateur productions are issued subject to the understanding that it shall be made clear in all advertising matter that the audience will witness an amateur performance; that the names of the authors of the plays shall be included in all programmes and that the integrity of the author's work will be preserved.

The Royalty Fee is subject to contract and subject to variation at the sole discretion of the author, Michael McEvoy.

NB. A licence issued to perform this play does not include permission to use any incidental music specified in this copy. Such permission must be separately obtained from the appropriate agent.

VIDEO-RECORDING OF
AMATEUR PRODUCTIONS

Please note that the copyright laws governing video-recording are extremely complex and that it should not be assumed that any play may be video-recorded for whatever purpose without first obtaining the permission of the appropriate agents. The fact that these plays are published by 49Knights, Independent Publishing House, Edinburgh & Cambridge, does not indicate that video rights are available or that 49Knights controls such rights.

FOREWORDS

The script of *An Act of Will* came to me at a strange point in my career. I'd been directing on the fringe, trying to write various things and was also working as a script editor and developer in film and television. And then I read this miniature, intense, detailed and nuanced script for one performer.

My memories of that time are that we spent nearly all the rehearsal time thinking about what connected the piece to the audience, trying to tease out what was theatrical. We rehearsed above a pub in whatever spare time we all had. It was wordy and detailed and slow.

Working on something like that opens up a different sort of theatrical experience. There are no bells or whistles or huge effects or climaxes. Instead you look for the music of words that paint pictures and tell a simple story.

I was particularly pleased when the play started to have a presence in international theatres because it felt almost perverse that such an intimate and detailed portrait could radiate out that far. But what it always had was love. The love of a character. The love of the words. And, perhaps most importantly, the love of the simple exchange between one performer and an audience.

– Steven Canny,
Director of the original production of *An Act of Will*

Michael McEvoy's play *An Act of Will* had one of its early performances in Canterbury, the birthplace of Christopher Marlowe, and it is, perhaps, the intriguing link between Shakespeare and Marlowe that makes this play so compelling.

Set at the imaginary latter end of his London career as a man of the theatre, William Shakespeare ruminates on his life and re-creates much of its creative progress in his and our imaginations. Set against a world of torture, religious intolerance, violence and prejudice (all too familiar even now) the unfolding drama of Shakespeare's career is presented through a clever mixture of direct address and role-play.

The play poses more questions than it provides answers and is all the stronger for that: the audience left the performance I witnessed pondering and fascinated: the writer dangles possibilities in front of us but never manipulates our thinking.

Shakespeare emerges as a complex and sometimes anxious character. He seems to be the product of a life of uncertainty, danger and rivalry: there are unspoken arrangements and secrets lying beneath the surface, and a strong performance by the one actor required in this play leads the audience through a tantalising labyrinth of doubts and certainties.

This play deserves to be widely read and performed.

– Ken Pickering,
Hon. Professor of Drama, University of Kent & Chairman of the
Marlowe Society

An Act of Will: The Secret Life of William Shakespeare

First performed at the Third International Theatre Festival, Lahore, Pakistan on Friday 12 November 1999.

Written & Performed by Michael McEvoy

Directed by Steven Canny

The play lasts approximately 90 mins

Notes on the text:

Notes on the text: SFX = sound and/or lighting effect.

Although lines in this play are frequently attributed to characters other than Shakespeare, only he is ever speaking. The words, including those of Will, his younger self, reflect the older Shakespeare's memories and recalled conversations, rather than giving an unbiased account of who said what and when within the drama.

Dedicated to my parents, Patrick McEvoy and Faith Noble, who gave me my love of Shakespeare.

[William SHAKESPEARE is sitting on a travelling trunk in the centre of the stage. He is seen in silhouette, in a classic pose, a sheet of paper in one hand and a quill pen in the other, deep in thought. The lights fade up. He holds the pose for a while. Then he stands and walks to the door left.]

{*as Shakespeare*} *[Calls.]* Anne! Anne! Are you in? Speak Anne if you hear.

[Chuckles at his misquotation.]

No sound? No word? Oh, well. Only to be expected.

[Looking again at paper as he speaks.]

I am twenty-four hours late, after all.

[Makes a final alteration to the paper.]

An unscheduled stop…

[He catches sight of the audience, newly aware of them.]

…in Oxford.

[Puts pen and paper on table left, and puts hand to his back as he straightens]

Well, that's finished.

[Steps forward, and executes an elaborate, curtain-call-type bow. Then, quieting the imagined applause, he steps further forward to make a curtain speech.]

Our revels now are ended. These our actors,
As I told you are…
[Corrects himself.]
As I foretold you, were all spirits and

An Act of Will

Are melted into air… into thin air…
And, like the baseless fabric of this vision…
…and so forth.

[Smiles.]

It has been such a life! Feted, celebrated, appearing at Court in front of His Majesty… and Hers… before his… majesty. Queen Elizabeth. Daughter of Henry VIII and Anne Boleyn. Ruling by the Divine Right of Kings, our first Protestant Queen. Declared a bastard by the Pope. Catholics informed that they… don't have to obey her commands! Achievements in the arts and sciences, in exploration and philosophy.

All in the face of the hawk-eyed, ever-watchful, puritanical Court of Star Chamber. Threats from Spain defeated. Threats of Catholic regicide defeated. The threat of chaos following Her Majesty's heirless – and, I imagine, hairless – demise defeated by the succession of His Majesty, King James. James the Sixth of Scotland, though the first that ever England in such an honour named.

Forgive me. It is our trick. We actors are so used to speaking other people's words that we quote or paraphrase by instinct… And, in my case, our own… words.

Such a life.

And what did I have by right, divine or otherwise? Oh, of course, my "reputation". The bubble reputation. As "England's Greatest Playwright". That.

[Again, switches on the Oscar-winning style and smile.]

> It has been such a... such a... strain.
> The trouble was, as soon as it started I was in it up to my neck. Stepped in so far returning were as tedious as go o'er. No, tedious is not the word. Suicidal. There was no going back.
>
> Sorry, you don't know what I'm talking about, do you? Well...

[Brave face: he's still got to hide the truth.]

> Neither do I. Frankly. A drink! That's what I need.

[Snaps fingers.]

> "Francis!"

[Snaps fingers again.]

> "Francis!" "Anon, anon, sir!"

[Laughs, then crosses to table and pours himself a drink.]

> Did you see that one?

[Mock pompous.]

> You have seen my plays, I take it? "My"... "works".

[Puts cup down and comes down to audience.]

> Ben Jonson told us the other day that he has kept all his play scripts neatly bound together. He said,
>
> After I've added a few more to the collection I'm

going to have them all published in a big folio
volume: Ben Jonson, His Works.

Someone murmured, "Poor old Ben. He doesn't
know the difference between work and play!"

Mmm? Why don't I do the same? Ah!

[He is at a loss as to how to answer this question for a moment.]

Well, it's not really my place to... I mean... er...
do you really think they're worth it?... Sorry, I
don't mean they're not good; they are.

*[His words become rapid and garbled as he tries to avoid blurting out that
which he should not.]*

In fact, they are the most marvellous set of look
you'll have to forgive me I've had a long journey
I'm... not expressing myself with the proper
caution – the proper...

[He stops, pauses, and gives a warm, friendly smile.]

Yes. Of course, you've seen my plays, otherwise,
you wouldn't be here. You've seen my plays and
now you want to meet the man who wrote them.
That's why you're... where?

[Turns upstage and takes in the set. Reassured.]

Stratford. Stratford. Stratford upon Avon.

[Goes to chair right and sits.]

A place where a man can kick off his boots and
drop the everlasting, never-ending, soul-
destroying... play-acting! And I don't mean on

the stage – that's the only place I could be anything near myself. That's dramatic irony if you like! Except it wasn't. The audience were the ones who were in the dark.

Oh. And are. Sorry.

You've got me at a difficult moment. I'm tired and off my guard. This is a turning point. In my life. No, it's not a turning point. It's the epilogue. Can an epilogue be a turning point? Probably not.

Who cares? The point, turning or otherwise, is this: I have come back to the place where I was born. It's an important moment. This is where I stay until I die. The beginning of... the end. A time to make one's peace with God. And that's not easy. Unless you do it the way my father did. There's another little secret. Hidden away in the rafters. A spiritual insurance policy... to make his peace with God.

And with the world? How do I make my peace with the world? Well, I think I've done that, quite frankly. After all, if it hadn't been for me... But who's to know? After we're all dead. Ah, yes, father, I was forgetting. God will know. And for the world... so many lives... hang on my... silence. It's a responsibility. I didn't ask for this.

[Consciously putting his worries aside.]

I need that drink. "Anon, anon, sir!"

[Goes back to table for his drink.]

Home at last for good. New Place. I bought this house sixteen years ago in 1597. One hundred and twenty pounds it cost. The second largest property in Stratford-upon-Avon. A home for Anne and Judith, and Susanna until she married, and now finally for me.

My father was a farmer. Yes, he did make gloves, but he also owned land, on which he kept cattle and sheep. And he owned property for rent. And, when I was born, he was the Mayor of Stratford. I was the third child, born 23rd April 1564. The eldest son, in a brood of eight, eventually.

[Puts down drink and comes down to audience.]

Oh, this town was a wonderful place to spend one's childhood. And the countryside surrounding it was rich and fertile. Dick Field and I used to snare rabbits to take home for supper. We both went to the Grammar School around the corner, where we learned to read and write in English and Latin and Greek. I was a poor scholar: "the whining schoolboy, with his satchel and shining morning face, creeping like snail unwillingly to school," as... I put it.

[Moving away.]

Dick was always questioning things. He never accepted at face value what he was taught at school. He had ideas about freedom of thought that were dangerous and exciting. We used to poach on the land of Sir Thomas Lucy, which got us a whipping more than once.

One day, the Earl of Leicester's men came to perform a play in the yard of an inn. Dick and I went to hear it. The yard was full of people milling about in front of a wooden stage set up against one wall, with a door at each side. And the galleries were full of people sitting eating and drinking. The place was abuzz with expectation. Suddenly a loud piece of music started up on the drums, shawm and sackbut. On came the actors and soon the whole place was ringing with the voice of James Burbage! I can't remember a thing about the play itself, but I was entranced by the magic of it. On my way home afterwards, I thought, I'd like to do that. One day I might be an actor.

From that time on, whenever the players came, Dick and I were there to see them. Warwick's men, Worcester's, Strange's – they all came to Stratford.

Then one day Dick told me he was leaving.

{as Dick} I'm going to London, Will. I've been offered an apprenticeship with a printer. I shall be able to see plays all the time there. They don't only perform in inn yards and market places. They've got proper playhouses in London, the Theatre and the Curtain.

{as Shakespeare} Father fell into debt. I had to leave school and help him with his work. My forays onto Sir Thomas Lucy's land became less a youthful prank and more a serious quest for food. Father sold off land to pay his debts – and he started to miss Council meetings.

The day my brother Edmund was born, Father sent me to deliver some gloves to a family in Temple Grafton. The door was opened by a girl of about sixteen. She had brown hair, green eyes and a beautiful smile. She told me her name was

Anne. Next time there was a delivery in the area, I volunteered for it. Soon I was visiting Anne twice or three times a week. We took long walks in the fields and woods. I was eighteen years old. It was the summer of 1582. And I was in love with Anne Whately.

Father got involved in a drunken brawl and was told to attend the court to apologize and guarantee to keep the peace in future. He refused. He was fined forty pounds. Things were going wrong for our family and I didn't understand why. And then it happened. I lost my virginity. And with it my youth. And with it my freedom.

Anne Hathaway of Shottery was eight years older than me. An experienced woman. She knew what she was doing. Oh, don't misunderstand. I was no unwilling participant. But this was more than a roll in the hay to her. As I said, she knew precisely what she was doing.

And I sensed this immediately. I felt I was in danger of losing something precious. Seized with a sense of urgency, I went straight over to Temple Grafton and asked Anne Whateley to marry me. And she said yes! It was the beginning of October. December 2nd to January 2nd is Advent, during which there can be no marriages. I had to move swiftly, but within a few weeks, we were given the necessary parental approval. And, on November 27th, we were issued with a marriage licence.

With the licence in my hand, at last, I could relax. I told my friends immediately, of course. And she told her friends. And my parents told theirs. And her parents told theirs. And that night two men from Shottery came knocking at our door.

Nature had taken her course and Anne Hathaway's insurance policy against a spinster's old age had paid its dividend.

The following morning, I was signing the register again, accompanied by these two gentlemen – who stood surety that I would go ahead with my marriage to Anne Hathaway. Forty pounds to indemnify the bishop, should Anne Whately assert her prior claim. They needn't have worried. When her parents found out that I had got Anne Hathaway with child, they were happy that their daughter had escaped the clutches of such a ne'er-do-well.

And so, I was married…

[Checks that he is not being overheard.]

…to the wrong Anne. Did I tell you she was eight years older than me? Well… She still is.

"…Let still the woman take
An elder than herself. So wears she to him.
So sways she level in her husband's heart."

So… she moved into our house. And six months later Susanna was born. Suddenly I was an adult, with responsibilities.

I worked hard in my father's business, desperately trying to keep it afloat, and all our mouths fed…

But still he got deeper into debt. He stopped attending Council meetings altogether and eventually he was dismissed from his post as alderman.

It was becoming increasingly clear that father was being persecuted because of his... He was a... *[Stops.]*

There's a problem here. How much do I tell you? To whom am I telling what I tell – you? What am I doing here? A soliloquy? Talking to... myself? An audience? Hamlet tells all. But so does the King. They neither of them believe that the audience will... snitch.

[He turns upstage, and speaks to himself, his back to the audience. It's an aside.]

Do I tell them? If I tell them about the religion, what about the rest... the vanishing trick? It's been easier to keep silent in London where others shared the secret, but now I am alone. Even my wife doesn't know the truth.

[Decides.]

Just the religion. Not the... other thing.

[Turning to audience.]

Sorry, I was just... thinking.

[Blurts it out.]

He was a Catholic. My father. We all were. So were my wife and her family. So, now you know. Well, I'm sorry, but you can't just change your religion overnight. Not even at the Queen's command.

Queen Elizabeth had once said that she sought no windows into men's souls. Catholics were tolerated so long as they were discreet. But as the Catholic plots against the Queen grew, so did the oppression, until eventually, the persecution of Catholics rivalled that of the Protestants under Mary.

And, in Stratford, the chief persecutor was... guess who? Sir Thomas Lucy. He was appointed "Commissioner with inquisitorial rights to investigate" the religious attitudes of... us, the people of Stratford.

In 1580, the saying of Mass had been banned. Anyone refusing to attend Protestant services paid a heavy fine. This was when my father started to miss Council meetings. He had begun to feel that he did not belong.
The following year, the year before I was married, two Jesuit Catholic priests turned up from Rome, Campion and Parsons. They brought with them a piece of paper. The idea was that, since we couldn't go to mass, we signed and kept this piece of paper stating our allegiance to the true faith. They called it a Spiritual Testament. Others might call it a suicide note.

I was the only member of the family who could read. I dutifully copied it out for my father. Father put his mark, sealed it and locked it away in a drawer. I told him,

{*as Will*}   If this gets discovered we're all finished.

{*as Shakespeare*}   In 1583, soon after Susanna was born, a deranged Catholic, John Somerville, rode into London, brandishing arms and sworn to assassinate the

Queen. He was captured and killed, but his accomplices escaped into Stratford. Sir Thomas Lucy was given the job of finding them.

{*as Will*}   [*Urgently.*] Father, Lucy's men are on their way! You must burn that document. Either it burns or we do. They're going from house to house, searching for evidence.

{*as his father*}   William, that document means more to me than my life – it is my hope of everlasting life.

{*as Will*}   For God's sake, Father...

{*as his father*}   Yes, William. For God's sake.

{*as Will*}   We'll have to hide it. Where? They might search under the floor, anywhere. In the roof!

{*as Shakespeare*}   I climbed up to the rafters and hid the document. Minutes later, Lucy's men arrived. After they had gone, I said,

{*as Will*}   I suppose we get it down again now.

{*as his father*}   No. Fix the wattle securely. Make sure the document is totally closed in.

{*as Will*}   Why not burn it in that case? What's the point of it up there where no one can read it?

{*as Shakespeare*}   Father looked at me sharply.

{*as his father*}   God can read it.

{*as Shakespeare*}   ...he said.

You know, I swear he thought God could read it

more clearly in the roof than if we'd put it under the floorboards. It's in the rafters of the old house still. I hope God's enjoying it.

[Sits right.]

My relationship with my wife was difficult. In the interest of a peaceful life I tried to hide, from myself as much as from her, the resentment I felt at losing Anne Whately and being pushed into a loveless marriage. I tried to make it work. I tried to make it less – loveless.

Worcester's men came to perform in Stratford. For the first time, I went with my wife to see the play. It was a revenge play written by a new young actor who had recently joined their company, Edward Alleyn. He played the part of a Danish prince who avenges his father's murder. He had a very powerful voice in the speeches where he swore "Revenge!", but he could also lower it to express deep sentiment.

That night, when we returned home after the play, was the night that the twins were conceived. They were born in January the following year, 1585. We named them after our friends Hamnet and Judith Sadler who acted as godparents. Two more mouths to feed.

I resumed my poaching, but it was becoming obvious to me that I would better feed my family if I left Stratford and found more lucrative work elsewhere.

One day my departure became a necessity. I shot one of Lucy's deer. A gamekeeper spotted me trying to drag the carcass into the bushes. I was

forced to abandon my booty and run. But I had
been spotted, identified, and I could by now
expect the full weight of the law to come down
upon me. I could have been hanged. I had to get
away. I left Stratford determined that my children
would never have to poach deer in order to eat.

[Rises, to centre.]

So it was that at twenty-nine years old, I arrived
in London for the first time. The city was a chaos
of shouts and smells and clattering. Everywhere I
turned I saw incident: an overturned barrow, a
screeching pig, a hollering chase of children. In
the middle of all this, I stood, travel-worn and
bewildered.

{*as Ned*}   Don't I know you?

{*as Shakespeare*} said a voice.

{*as Will*}   Er... I don't think so. No, I'm sorry, but I don't
                    remember you.

{*as Ned*}   Warwickshire?

{*as Will*}   Er – yes, I'm from Warwickshire.

{*as Ned*}   Whereabouts?

{*as Will*}   Stratford upon Avon.

{*as Ned*}   Of course, Stratford! I knew your face as soon as
                    I saw you. Your name... now don't tell me... it's
                    John... is it? No... Sorry, it's gone...?

[He is given the name.]

Will. Of course! Will. Why did I think it was John?

{*as Will*} You might have been thinking of my father, John Shakespeare.

{*as Ned*} Of course, silly of me. Well, I'm so pleased to see you again, Will Shakespeare. You remember me, Ned Fletcher, of course. We have much to talk about. I long to hear about the people back in Stratford. Your father – he is well? I wonder if you'd care to join me for a drink in that ordinary over the way?

{*as Shakespeare*} I was thirsty after my journey. The tavern was packed with traders of all kinds. We found a table and Ned ordered two cups of ale.

Behind Ned, the door opened and I saw two extraordinary men enter the tavern. One was a large, evil-looking man, with tattoos covering both arms. He would have seemed of startling appearance without his smaller companion. But with him! This man's clothing was entirely of a bright green – goose-turd green. His red hair was greased to a sharp pyramid atop his head, with his equally red beard greased to a point likewise, a single pearl hanging from the tip. These two visions settled themselves with their drinks on a bench by the wall, and the red and green man was soon busily scribbling in a notebook.

[Sits left.]

Ned was saying...

{*as Ned*} I am sorry to hear dear old John Shakespeare is finding things difficult. But maybe I'm in a position to help his son to fill his purse.

{*as Shakespeare*} Over Ned's shoulder, I noticed that the red-haired man was listening to our conversation.

{*as Ned*} What I have in mind could prove lucrative for both of us. But it will require a bit of investment. I don't suppose you've much money with you?

{*as Will*} I have a little.

{*as Shakespeare*} I said.

{*as Ned*} In that case, you're in luck.

{*as Will*} Actually, I'm trying to find an old friend who might help me into a job. His name's Dick Field.

{*as Ned*} Dick Field? Oh, yes, of course, I know him.

{*as Greene*} Of course you do...

{*as Shakespeare*} ...said a voice. I looked up. It was the red-haired man.

{*as Greene*} And I dare say you will be personally acquainted with anyone else the gentleman cares to mention.

{*as Shakespeare*} Ned gulped his drink down and slammed his cup onto the table.

[Rises.]

He stood up and looked the red-haired man in the eye.

{*as Ned*} Your days are numbered, Master Greene. We'll put paid to your scribbling, you'll see.

{*as Shakespeare*} And he marched out without giving me another glance. The red-haired man looked at me and smiled.

{*as Greene*} Welcome to London. You seem confused. And so you might. I have just rescued your purse from that gentleman's clutches.

{*as Shakespeare*} My hand went to my purse.

{*as Greene*} Oh, don't worry. Our friend was not a cutpurse. He and his kind have subtler methods than that.

{*as Will*} But he seemed to know me.

{*as Greene*} This is London. Things are not always what they seem to be. A coney catcher. A notorious one. London is full of them. Allow me to introduce myself. Robert Greene. *[Sits]*

{*as Will*} My name is Will Shakespeare sir. That man, he threatened you...

{*as Greene*} These coney catchers are always warning me against publishing my pamphlets exposing their tricks. I used not to take their threats seriously. But nowadays...

[Points.]

Cutting Ball here used to be a highwayman, now he's my bodyguard. They are afraid of him for his brawn and me for my brain. Together we shall make life very hard for these parasitical caterpillars. So, Will Shakespeare, what brings you to London?

{*as Will*} I'm looking for a job... as an actor.

[Rises and confides in audience.]

{*as Shakespeare*} It was the first time I had actually admitted, even
                    to myself, that that was what I wanted to do.

[Returning to his seat.]

                    My companion was scowling.

{*as Will*}   You don't approve of actors?

{*as Greene*}   Caterpillars, the lot of them. It is we writers who
                    put the words into their mouths. But there be
                    some actors, overblown in their estimation of
                    their own worth, who think they can write the
                    plays that they strut on stage! Puppets who think
                    that they can pull their own strings. Have you
                    ever heard of one Edward Alleyn?

{*as Will*}   Oh, yes, I saw him act with Worcester's men in
                    Stratford seven years ago. I thought him very fine.

{*as Greene*}   Did you? He is a ranting scene-shaker. He is now
                    performing in the plays of Christopher Marlowe
                    at the Rose, acclaimed the leading actor of our
                    time. A new Roscius. Come. I'll show you where
                    you can find your friend Dick Field.

[Rises and crosses to centre.]

{*as Shakespeare*} Dick was in his print shop, binding a book of
                    poetry. He looked up from his work. It was several
                    seconds before he recognized me.

{*as Dick*}   Will Shakespeare! Ha! I knew one day you would
                    walk in through that door. I knew it. Come in,
                    come in and welcome.

{*as Shakespeare*} I told him what had brought me to London.

{*as Dick*} Oh, yes – Sir Thomas Lucy! We hear of his exploits down here. He is a very assiduous hunter of Catholic priests. It's good to know you Catholics are taking his venison in return. Oh, don't be alarmed. There is freedom of thought in this house. Our task here is the opening of minds, not the closing of mouths. We publish many, many books. This is our next one. It's a poem by Christopher Marlowe.

{*as Will*} Marlowe...

{*as Shakespeare*} I said.

{*as Will*} ...That's the second time I've heard his name today.

{*as Shakespeare*} I told him of my meeting with Robert Greene.

{*as Dick*} Greene is an embittered man. He resents Edward Alleyn writing plays for himself. In fact, he resents the grammar-school men writing plays at all. *[Imitating Greene's voice]* "It's a university man's work!"

But he needs more than his university degree before he can hope to compete with the great Kit Marlowe. You must come with me tomorrow to hear one of his plays. Meanwhile, we must find you a bed.

{*as Shakespeare*} Tamburlaine the Great was unlike any play I had ever seen. The beauty of the language, the way Christopher Marlowe used words to conjure up whole new worlds in your imagination... fulfilling the promise made at the beginning of the play,

that he would do far, far more than had been
previously done by playwrights:

From jigging veins of rhyming mother-wits,
And such conceits as clownage keeps in pay,
We'll lead you to the stately tent of war,
Where you shall hear the Scythian Tamburlaine
Threatening the world with high astounding
terms,
And scourging kingdoms with his conquering
sword.
View but his picture in this tragic glass,
And then applaud his fortunes as you please.

[Claps enthusiastically.]

And we did applaud, long and loud! It was
magnificent! Alleyn was magnificent! But, as
Greene had said, it was the playwright who had
given him his power.

Dick and I resumed our play-going together. We
saw The Jew of Malta by Christopher Marlowe.
And Greene's Orlando Furioso. The big
passionate speeches in Orlando seemed poor
imitations of those of Tamburlaine. But it was, all
the same, a well-made play.

Unlike Alleyn's Faire Em, the Miller's Daughter
of Manchester, which was a poor piece of work
compared with the others. There were no less
than twelve of Alleyn's plays currently in the
repertoire at the Rose, including a revised version
of the Hamlet that I'd seen in Stratford. With
Marlowe's pearls eked out with Alleyn's dross,
there was little that Greene could hope for in
earning a living from the writing of plays.

But Greene did have a new play at the Rose, that month – A Knack to Know a Knave. There were a great number of noisy apprentices in the pit. They had chosen the Rose as their assembly point before setting off across the river to the Marshalsea prison to protest the arrest of one of their fellows. When they got there, they were set upon by the Marshal's men using daggers and cudgels. The resulting riot brought a swift reaction from the Privy Council. The playhouses were closed for the rest of the summer.

I went back to Stratford. But I had learned one thing from my meeting with Robert Greene: there was money to be had as an actor.

When I returned to London in September, Robert Greene was dead. His bodyguard had been hanged at Tyburn for highway robbery. And they said Greene had died of a surfeit of Rhenish wine and herrings. It sounded unlikely to me. I remembered the coney catcher's threat.

Greene was dead – but his voice not silenced. He had tried to borrow money from the manager of the Rose and been turned down.

[Takes pamphlet out of trunk.]

He wrote this pamphlet, published shortly after his death, blaming Marlowe and Alleyn for squeezing him out of his means of earning a living. His attack on Marlowe was particularly insidious:

{*as Greene*}   *[Reads]* Wonder not, thou famous gracer of Tragedians, that Greene, who hath said with thee there is no God, should now give glory unto

God's greatness: he hath spoken to me with a voice of thunder. He is a God that can punish enemies. Why should thy excellent wit, God's gift, be so blinded, that thou should'st give no glory to the giver? O peevish folly!

{*as Shakespeare*} There was no mistaking that this was directed at Marlowe, and it amounted to an accusation of the crime of atheism. Greene then addresses his fellow writers, warning them against actors:

{*as Greene*} [Reads] ...those Puppets that spake from our mouths, those Anticks garnished in our colours. Trust them not: for there is an upstart Crow, beautified with our feathers, that with his Tiger's heart wrapt in a Player's hide, supposes he is as well able to bombast out a blank verse as the best of you: and being an absolute Johannes fac totum, is in his own conceit the only Shake-scene in a country.

{*as Shakespeare*} The True Tragedy of Richard, Duke of York had been a big success at the Rose. Edward Alleyn was famed for his delivery of the line, "A tiger's heart wrapt in a woman's hide". So there was no doubt as to the identity of this "tiger's heart wrapt in a player's hide".

Alleyn and Marlowe both demanded an apology from the publisher – it was too late to get one from Greene himself.

[Taking out a paper which is tucked into the back of the pamphlet.]

Though Marlowe had received the greatest and most dangerous libel, the suggestion of atheism, the publisher made apology only to Alleyn. [Reads.] "With neither of them that take offence was I acquainted, and with one of them I care not if I never be. For the other, I am as sorry as if the original fault had been mine."

The libel against Marlowe remained. He stood publicly accused of atheism.

[Puts pamphlet on table.]

There was an atmosphere of discontent in London. The general unease about the plague found expression in attacks on foreigners. The city had many traders from the Netherlands.

A placard was nailed up on the wall of the Dutch Church, threatening violence against the "strangers". Fifty-three lines of doggerel verse, signed at the bottom, "Tamburlaine". Marlowe was frequently referred to by the name of his most famous creation.

The Privy Council sent out officers to find the author of this paper.

But they didn't arrest Marlowe – not yet. They knew he wasn't the author. They wanted evidence against him first. They arrested the playwright Thomas Kyd. And they stretched him on the rack, waving a heretical document at him that they claimed to have found in his room. Kyd said that it was not his and if it was found in his room it must be Marlowe's because they used to share the room together.

Christopher Marlowe was placed under arrest.

[Stops. Looks questioningly from face to face in audience.]

Mmm? What about my plays? You want to hear about Romeo and Juliet, Macbeth, and so forth? Well, I'm sorry, but you'll just have to be patient. I've got to reach the age of thirty before you get my first written work, Venus and Adonis. You can't hurry genius.

And besides, I haven't decided who you are yet. A lot depends on that. On that depends which story I tell you.

[Thinks about it. An idea occurs to him. He takes out a silk handkerchief and performs a conjuring trick.]

Melted into air... into thin air.

[Reveals that the handkerchief has vanished. Takes a bow. The audience reaction decides him.]

You're an audience! I can handle that.

[Gets drink and raises cup to them.]

Your health.

[Drinks. Then he comes down centre and announces:]

The Making of a Bard.

At the age of twenty-five, was I reading Ovid? No, I was a poor country craftsman metamorphosing a calfskin into a glove.

At twenty-seven was I perfecting iambic pentameter? No, I was struggling to ensure the feet of my children were shod.

At fifty am I surrounded by Ovid, Holinshead,

Plutarch? No, barely a book to my name, but…

[Opens trunk and takes out a scroll of paper bound in red ribbon.]

I have just invested in some land outside Stratford. That is progress.

[Chummily.]

You don't want a conventional story! No, surely not!

In a soliloquy, there is no reason to lie. Does that mean that what is spoken is the truth? Ye-es, but only the truth within the play. And the play itself is an invention.

[Sits on trunk] I shall tell you a story. After all, you are an audience. You must expect to hear invention on the stage. "If this were played upon a stage now, I could condemn it as an improbable fiction." Fabian. Twelfth Night. That got a big laugh. They loved that. A kind of in-joke, for a sophisticated audience. Twelfth Night was full of them. More than any other play.

The Romans had an annual feast of Saturnalia, where the slaves reversed roles with their masters. For one day of the year, they changed clothes and the slaves gave the orders. The glimpse of chaos that preserves order. This feast of Saturnalia has come down to us as Twelfth Night.

[Rises.]

And in 1601, at Whitehall, in front of the Queen, on the sixth of January – Twelfth Night – we performed… Twelfth Night! With the Florentine

Duke, Orsino, as the guest of honour.

[With a gesture he casts an audience member in the role.]

And onstage...

[Indicates himself.]

...another Orsino!

He starts the play. He plays a whole scene as the handsome, love-lorn, and so far unnamed, Duke:

[Sits on trunk.]

If music be the food of love, play on,
Give me excess of it, that, surfeiting,
The appetite may sicken, and so die.
That strain again, it had a dying fall:
O, it came o'er my ear like the sweet sound
That breathes upon a bank of violets,
Stealing and giving odour.

[Rises abruptly.]

Enough, no more. I can't do it anything approaching justice. But you should have heard Burbage deliver it. He was an actor. Richard Burbage, that is. James was his father.

And Orsino – the real one, sitting there, rapt. And Her Majesty...

[Another audience member.]

...visibly proud – of us. Oh, it made you feel good.

And then, the name. The in-joke. The first one

of the play, really. The Olivia-Elizabeth pun doesn't sink in for a while – not till we've heard his name.

This Duke plays a whole scene and leaves the stage, and we still don't know his name! Viola comes on, with the Captain – played by me! – and the rest of the crew, wet. And we hear that she's shipwrecked in Illyria.

"Who governs here?" she says.

"A noble duke, in nature as in name." replies the Captain.

"What is his name?"

"Orsino."

Big laugh!

And she repeats it, for those who missed it.

"Orsino!"

More laughter.

"I have heard my father name him.
He was a bachelor then."

"And so is now, or was so very late;
For but a month ago I went from hence,
And then 'twas fresh in murmur
That he did seek the love of fair Olivia."

"Olivia? What's she?"

"A virtuous maid."

It was really cheeky – but they loved it! Well, it was Twelfth Night – Saturnalia. We, her Majesty's servants, were given licence to do... what you will.

It was a first night to remember.

I was going to tell you something. Oh, that's right, the truth. Or, a story. What you will.

[Pause. Sits. With emphasis.]

Orsino's visit was kept secret until a few days beforehand when the Master of Revels brought the command for our performance on Twelfth Night.

And I am supposed to have written that play – and our actors are supposed to have... In a matter of days?

[Pause. Rises. Goes to table and gets himself another drink.]

[To himself.] I am blind on the edge of a precipice, like Gloucester. Do I jump? It will take an act of will. I see the consequences. I see four centuries of men's eyes gazing at me in defiant disbelief. I see academe foaming at the mouth in fury...

Well, let them rage – or laugh. Laugh is more likely. Maybe it is no precipice at all, but plain ground. *[Makes the decision. Addresses audience]* I shall tell you the story and you can condemn it as an improbable fiction. Or not. You can do what you will with it.

[Drinks. Puts down cup and sits on trunk.]

A week after Marlowe was arrested Dick Field came to see me. He looked as if he hadn't slept for a week.

{*as Dick*}   Will, I want you to do something for me. You have heard of Kit Marlowe's arrest?

{*as Shakespeare*} I told him I had.

{*as Dick*}   Marlowe's patron, Thomas Walsingham, wants to see you tomorrow. Will you come with me to his house in Scadbury in Kent?

{*as Shakespeare*} The following day we travelled to Scadbury accompanied by a man who introduced himself as a servant of Thomas Walsingham. His name was Ingram Frizer.

It was the most magnificent house I had ever set foot in.

Walsingham said...

{*as Walsingham*} There's someone I want you to meet.

{*as Shakespeare*} A well-dressed young man came over to me and put out his hand.

{*as Marlowe*}   Christopher Marlowe.

{*as Shakespeare*} ...he said.

[*Rises.*]

{*as Will*}   William Shakespeare. I thought you had been arrested.

{*as Marlowe*}   I have to report daily to the Court of Star

Chamber. My bail runs out in a few days.

{as Shakespeare}   Walsingham said,

{as Walsingham}   I simply wanted you two to meet, Will, because I think you might be able to help.

{as Will}   In what way?

{as Walsingham}   We can concern ourselves with that later. For now, I think Kit has something to say.

{as Marlowe}   Yes. I want you to know that whatever charges are brought against me, the truth is that I have always served my country and my Queen loyally. I have risked my life on many occasions. I served against the Spanish Armada. I was instrumental in uncovering the traitor Anthony Babington.

The Court of Star Chamber are anxious to break up a circle of friends of which I am a member, as is Thomas here. Our enemies call us atheists, conjurers and the like. They call us the School of Night. But it is not darkness, but enlightenment that we seek. Such seekers after knowledge are imprisoned or done to death by ignorant but powerful men.

{as Shakespeare}   I nodded.

{as Will}   "I hold there is no sin but ignorance."

{as Shakespeare}   ...I said

{as Marlowe}   [*Surprised.*] You know my Jew of Malta?

{as Will}   Also Tamburlaine. Anything I can do to help the author of such works I will perform with a glad

heart.

{*as Shakespeare*} And that was the end of our meeting. Shortly after, Dick and I returned to London.

[Crosses upstage, and turns.]

The following day, 30th May 1593, Christopher Marlowe was dead.

It was a shock. And the manner of his death, when I heard it, was another shock. Walsingham's servant, our travelling companion of the previous day, Ingram Frizer, had been arrested for his murder.

Frizer and Marlowe, and two other men, Nicholas Skeres and Robert Poley, had rented a room in a house in Deptford for the day. Why? Well, no one really questioned that at the time, because the death that took place in that little room was so shocking that questions of that kind were, shall we say, upstaged by it.

Towards the end of the day a quarrel broke out between Marlowe and Frizer over who was to pay the reckoning, the bill. But it seems this argument was somehow resolved, or at least, no longer in progress, when the deed was done. Because Poley, Frizer and Skeres were sitting on a bench at the table, with Frizer in the middle. Marlowe was resting on a bunk.

[Acting out the scene.]

Marlowe crept up behind them, pulled Frizer's knife out of its sheath, and struck him twice on the head with the butt of it. Frizer struggled to retrieve the knife and... Marlowe fell, dead, with the knife in his right eye.

I was staggered by this piece of news. Having only met both killer and victim the previous day for the first time, I found it impossible to visualize those two men playing out this violent scene together. Who were the other two, Poley and Skeres? Why had these four men met together to spend the day in this room? It was like to have been the last day of Marlowe's freedom. What charges was he facing? They might have been so grave as to deprive him of his freedom forever. Or his life.

I went into a tavern and bought myself a drink.

[Sits on trunk.]

By the time I had finished it, I had become convinced that Marlowe's death had been planned. Maybe it was this School of Night that he had told me of. After all, his arrest had resulted from evidence extracted from Kyd under torture. Maybe his fellows in the School of Night had feared for their safety should Marlowe himself come under torture. This must have been the case! Walsingham was a member of the circle – and it was his servant, Frizer, who had stabbed Marlowe to death! The other two men were part of the plot. Maybe the story was true but reversed. Maybe Marlowe was jammed in between Poley and Skeres, and it was Frizer who came up behind Marlowe and stabbed him in the eye. Why in the eye, not in the back? Because it had to look like an accident. Poley and Skeres were there to back up Frizer's plea of self-defence. The more I thought about it, the more certain I was that I had hit upon the truth of the matter.

Yet another writer murdered, and yet again the murderer would get away with it.

I felt duty-bound to do something about it. I finished my drink and hurried round to Dick's print shop.

{*as Dick*}   Hello, Will. I was expecting you. You've come to tell me of Marlowe's death.

{*as Will*}   Yes...

{*as Shakespeare*}   I said, surprised at his casual manner.

{*as Will*}   I think it was a plot. I think Walsingham's behind it.

{*as Walsingham*}   Right on both counts.

{*as Shakespeare*}   said a voice.

[Swings round.]

{*as Shakespeare*}   Walsingham was sitting in a chair by the door! Immediately I thought: Dick's in it, too!

I must have gone white because Walsingham then said,

{*as Walsingham*}   Don't worry. You're in no danger. Certainly, no more than the rest of us. Please sit down. We have much to plan. Yesterday, you promised Kit that you would be willing to do anything to help him.

[Sits on trunk.]

{*as Will*}   It's too late for that now.

{*as Shakespeare*}   I said.

{*as Walsingham*}   No, it isn't.

{*as Shakespeare*}   He closed the door. Dick came over and sat facing me. In a low, emphatic voice he said,

{*as Dick*}   Kit is not dead.

{*as Shakespeare*}   I felt a rush to my head. This was the second such shock that day. First, he was dead, then he wasn't. Such welcome and unwelcome news at once...

Walsingham told me an astonishing story.

[*Rises.*]

{*as Walsingham*}   If Marlowe had returned to the Court of Star Chamber today, he would have faced the most appalling charges. We don't yet know what they would have been, but we can be certain that heresy would have been one of them. They would have resulted in our finest playwright and poet being tortured and horribly executed.

In the process he would have been forced to swear to any falsehood his torturers had put to him, betraying me and the other members of the School of Night. You have no doubt worked that out already, which is why you have come here believing that I murdered him.

Dick here, and I, and my servant Frizer, who faces at this moment the charge of murder, and others, are all in mortal danger. We have put ourselves in this position by choice – in order to save our friend. I will tell you precisely what took place yesterday in Dame Elinor Bull's house in

Deptford.

The Dame's cousin is a gentlewoman of my acquaintance at Court. She recommended the good Dame to me for two admirable qualities. One, she is completely trustworthy, and two, her house backs onto the river. Yesterday morning, Ingram Frizer went to Deptford with Marlowe. They and Skeres and Poley met at the Dame's house. Skeres and Poley are both men who used to work for my cousin, Sir Francis Walsingham. They, like Marlowe, were part of his secret service. At a prearranged moment in the morning, a boat pulled up, Marlowe, heavily disguised, stepped on board. And away he went.

The remaining three men stayed in the room and the garden for eight hours in all. Giving Marlowe time to get well away, and themselves time to perfect their story in every detail. During the afternoon, another boat arrived, bearing the body of an executed criminal. In order to aid the deception, it was decided that the knife wound should be in the face. The inquest takes place tomorrow. It should be a formality.

{*as Shakespeare*} I sat stunned. There must be a flaw in this outrageous plot.

{*as Walsingham*} The body will be buried in an unmarked grave in Deptford churchyard. Frizer will spend an uncomfortable few weeks in jail, but the self-defence plea should secure him a release. I will pull the necessary strings.

{*as Shakespeare*} I felt I was dreaming.

{*as Will*} What about Marlowe? Where's he gone?

{*as Walsingham*} Italy.

[*Sits.*]

{*as Shakespeare*} There was a long silence. It really was a
                    dangerous, daring plot! It was like the plot of a
                    play. But it was far more improbable than any
                    invention I had heard on a stage.

                    Then it struck me! And when it did, it was like a
                    physical blow to the body.

[*Rises, angrily.*]

                    Why the devil have you told me this? Why did
                    you have to drag me into it? Why did you take me
                    to Scadbury to meet Marlowe? And why are you
                    telling me now of your conspiracy? You've made
                    me as guilty as the rest of you!

{*as Walsingham*} [*Calmly.*] No. You are not guilty of anything. You
                    can walk out of here and tell the world. You are
                    free to go. No one will stop you. You are not guilty
                    until you decide to stay silent.

{*as Shakespeare*} I thought for a while. No, I didn't. I pretended to
                    think for a while. I let them believe, just for a
                    moment, that I might betray them. I took my
                    time, punishing them for putting me in this
                    position. Eventually, I said...

{*as Will*}   You have my silence.

[*Pause. He walks upstage slowly. Turns. Quietly.*]

                    Why have you dragged me into this?

{*as Shakespeare*} Walsingham said,

{*as Walsingham*} Think of Kit now. He's going on a long journey into exile. His experience as a secret agent will help him. But what will he do? He must find himself some sort of employment out there. He knows that he has my undying support. I am still his patron. He is still my poet. More than this. He is still my dear, dear friend. But a poet is not a poet unless he writes poems, a playwright not a playwright unless he writes plays. If he continues to write plays, who will produce them?

{*as Shakespeare*} Dick said...

{*as Dick*} You and Kit are exactly the same age, Will. It is reasonable to suppose you will both live to roughly the same age. Kit has a lifetime of playmaking still in him.

{*as Shakespeare*} Walsingham said...

{*as Walsingham*} What he has achieved is superb. They are the finest plays that have ever been written. But there are greater still to come.

{*as Shakespeare*} Dick said...

{*as Dick*} You are unknown in London. You told me you wanted a career on the stage. Now's your chance.

{*as Shakespeare*} Walsingham said...

{*as Walsingham*} I can secure you a place as an actor at the Theatre in Shoreditch.

{*as Will*} James Burbage's Theatre!

{*as Shakespeare*} ...I said.

{*as Walsingham*}   Yes. This is what we want. You take up this offer
                    as actor, shareholder and playbroker with James
                    Burbage's company. And you supply them with
                    scripts – all sorts of scripts – from many
                    playwrights, but particularly from Marlowe.

{*as Shakespeare*} Dick said,

{*as Dick*}   But you don't say they're by Marlowe.

{*as Will*}   Well, whom do I say they're by?

{*as Shakespeare*} They exchanged a look.

{*as Dick*}   Say you wrote them.

{*as Will*}   [*Bursts out laughing.*] I can't do that!

{*as Dick*}   Why not?

{*as Shakespeare*} ...said Dick. I looked at Walsingham.

{*as Walsingham*}   Why not?

{*as Shakespeare*} ...he said. [*With a slight shrug*] And that was that.
                    Except that, as I was leaving, Walsingham came
                    over and shook my hand.

{*as Walsingham*}   I can't thank you enough for doing this for my
                    dear friend. It is a very heavy burden to place on
                    you. It would make me happy if you would accept
                    a sum of money as well, as a token of my
                    gratitude. If you will make the necessary
                    preparations in the next week or two to take
                    possession of it, I shall arrange for you to receive
                    a thousand pounds.

[*Throws the audience a look. Then he opens the trunk and pulls out a framed picture of Marlowe. Indicates inscription.]*

{*as Shakespeare*} Marlowe's personal motto: *[Reads]* Quod me nutrit me destruit. "What nourishes me destroys me." In the pay of the Government from a very early age, when he was at university before he wrote his first play. And then, his reputation destroyed by the machinery of state.

[Hangs picture on wall, right.]

"What nourishes me destroys me".

We moved swiftly.

[Sits on trunk.]

Venus and Adonis had been registered at the Stationer's Office in April, with no author's name attached to it. It was ready for publication. Twelve days after Christopher Marlowe's death in Deptford, William Shakespeare's first poem was published – with a dedication to the Earl of Southampton, who had passed on to me Walsingham's thousand pounds.

I was rich. And I had a career as an actor.

My family started to feel the benefits immediately. My father was able to pay all his debts and begin to reclimb the social ladder.

[Rises.]

Eventually, we heard the charges against Marlowe. One Richard Baines had been assigned the task of concocting a charge sheet. The charges were heresy, blasphemy, homosexuality, forgery. All capital crimes. And all, apparently, boasted of publicly by Marlowe to anyone who would listen. A man desperately trying to get himself tortured and executed could not have done better. The document was clearly a work of complete fiction.

It ended with the recommendation that Marlowe's mouth be stopped. It was now up to me to make sure it wasn't.

[Opens trunk and takes out a sheet of paper.]

Walsingham soon started receiving more sonnets from Marlowe to add to his collection, composed on the long, lonely journey to Italy.

[Sits and reads.]

Weary with toil, I haste me to my bed,
The dear repose for limbs with travel tired,
But then begins a journey in my head
To work my mind, when body's work's expired;
For then my thoughts (from far where I abide)
Intend a zealous pilgrimage to thee,
And keep my drooping eyelids open wide,
Looking on darkness that the blind do see:
Save that my soul's imaginary sight
Presents thy shadow to my sightless view,
Which like a jewel (hung in ghastly night)
Makes black night beauteous, and her old face new.
Lo, thus by day my limbs, by night my mind,
For thee, and for myself, no quiet find.

[Puts paper on table and crosses down to audience.]

The plays came rapidly: The Two Gentlemen of

Verona, Love's Labour's Lost, Richard III. Richard Burbage was brilliant as Richard III. In spite of the fact that the character is so evil, he managed to get the whole audience on his side! – much as Alleyn had done as Tamburlaine – the difference being that there was humour in Richard's character. The audience laughed with him. Under the new patronage of the Lord Chamberlain, the company at the Theatre began a period when they would produce the finest plays the world had known.

Marlowe had settled in Verona and was busily snapping up unconsidered trifles and making masterpieces out of them. He really could turn the basest dross into pure gold. He had the Midas touch. His alchemy was at its most astonishing in his transformation of that first play by Edward Alleyn that I had seen in Stratford. After performing it at the Rose, Alleyn had abandoned it. But Marlowe had seen the play's potential, and now he rewrote it for us. We performed Hamlet at Newington Butts. It was a dreadful playhouse, no one liked performing there. But the play was a success.

Keeping up the pretence was a constant strain. Actors would come to me with their scripts and question me on the meaning of a line. If I didn't know the answer I would just have to bluff my way out of it! Worst was when they wanted me to rewrite a line. This was torment. Usually, I struck a pose as the offended poet and implied that the truth of the line required that it be spoken thus and no other way.

The arrival of a new play from Italy was an exciting moment. On receiving the message, I would excuse myself from my duties at the Theatre and set forth for Scadbury, where Walsingham would wine and dine me and we would read through the new script together. He would give me a bed for the night and I would spend the following day scrupulously copying out the new play. When the task was complete, Walsingham would take one last, loving look through Marlowe's original manuscript. Then we would stand in silence as it burned on the fire.

These were moments of calm in a busy life. The company rehearsed in the mornings and performed in the afternoons. The evenings were taken up with book-keeping, repairs and maintenance, drawing up plans for new productions, correspondence, and so forth. You might have thought people would look at my daily schedule and ask how I found the time to write the plays. They didn't. Not once. There was a reason for this. The plays were too good.

I had a "gift", they said. This "gift" gradually became a "genius". Because of this genius the words were seen as just flowing out of my pen. The greater the writer, the logic goes, the easier the writing. People are quite happy with this paradox.

Every so often I would turn up with a bundle of sheets of paper under my arm and hand over to my fellow actors a truly great piece of writing as if it were merely something I had dashed off in a few idle moments. They commented on the fact that there were never any blots or crossings out. But this merely reinforced their preconceptions.

Ben Jonson, on the other hand, found much that

should have been crossed out. Jonson was a writer. He knew the toil that went into creating a piece for the stage, and he was truly astonished at my seeming facility. He teased me over my lack of learning whilst experiencing enormous difficulties in reconciling this lack with the classical references that peppered the plays.

I was posing as living proof that Robert Greene had been wrong and that a grammar school boy could rival even the great Christopher Marlowe. If Marlowe had the Midas touch, I resembled Midas in another way. My ass's ears were hidden beneath the crown I had usurped from Marlowe. I was haunted by Greene's resentful ghost, whispering my secret from the very grass I walked upon.

[Sits on trunk.]

The Lord Chamberlain's men flourished. Will Kempe was a superb clown, though he tended to ad lib. and share jokes with the audience. This was resented by some. Kempe would often lead the jigs at the end of a play. John Hemminges was a solid, but not a great actor. He had a slight stutter, which lent an element of suspense to the dullest speech. And Richard Burbage was a well-built man, a fine leading actor to rival Edward Alleyn at the Rose. And he was a noted painter.

[Rises, distressed.]

I received some news from home. My only son, Hamnet, was in bed with a high fever. The doctor was not hopeful. I saddled my horse and raced to Stratford.

[Crosses to upstage of the trunk and turns.]

I was too late. My son was dead. He was eleven years old.

We buried him in the churchyard. The dirt thudded onto the coffin, eventually hiding it completely. All that remained of him was a picture in my mind's eye.

Is that true? Is that all there is of him? An image moulded out of memory by grief? No, he must be in heaven.

The atheists would not have it so. No God, no heaven. Richard Baines had claimed that Marlowe had stated that ancient writings had survived proving that men had lived ten thousand years before the date of Adam claimed by Christianity. What if this were so? Would it mean that God did not create the world and everything in it? That the world had somehow come about by accident? Out of nothing? No. Nothing will come of nothing.

I see my son in my mind's eye. Where does that image go when I, too, am dead?

Does history only exist in our memories? And in books? What if I burn a book? The only book that tells of a historical event? Does that mean it never happened?

My son exists in my memory. So does Kit Marlowe. But our memories die with us. The memory of the world lives on in books. And what will the books tell the world about us? That Christopher Marlowe was a blasphemer, who died while attempting murder. That William Shakespeare was a writer of genius. If for, say, four hundred years all the world believes this to be so, is it not, therefore, the truth? If not, where is the truth?

[Looks up.]

It is up there, written in the rafters. God can read the truth.

A few weeks after my son's death, my father was awarded the coat of arms he had so longed for. It meant so much to him, and so little to me. The justification for it was my pre-eminence in the theatre... and the fact that I had paid a vast sum to the Garter King of Arms.

[Opens trunk.]

Here it is.

[Produces it.]

See the spear?

[Shakes it.]

See? And the motto. Irony of ironies, the motto: Non Sans Droit, "Not without right". Not without right? What had I done in the theatre to deserve it? And the money I used to pay for it? What had I done to deserve that?

[Hangs it on back wall.]

And it is supposed to be worn proudly by succeeding generations, handed down from father to son. I had just buried my only son. "Not without right." Well, there it is, a mere scutcheon.

In 1597 at the Swan, Ben Jonson's play The Isle of Dogs caused a riot. Ben was put under arrest and the Privy Council closed all the playhouses.

This was when I bought this house in New Place. I realized how suddenly retirement might come.

With the Theatre closed, we toured. There had been a clause in our lease on the Theatre that the building should belong to us if it were removed from the land it stood on before the lease had lapsed. While we toured, the lease ran out. When we returned to London in October, we found that the landowner had fenced off the Theatre. He threatened to prosecute us for trespass if we set one foot on his land.

We put on Ben Jonson's new play at the Curtain, Every Man in His Humour. But any thought that prison had mellowed Jonson was soon dispelled. He quarrelled with an actor, Gabriel Spencer, and challenged him to a duel. Next thing we knew, Jonson was back in prison on a charge of murder. He was found guilty and sentenced to death. My future was less certain.

At any time, I could find myself with no income. The company had bought a patch of land on the south bank of the Thames, near the Rose, but we couldn't perform in a field. Even if we had a new playhouse, apart from the constant threat of closure, there was always the danger that the scripts would stop coming. On a visit to Stratford I made an investment in the town's thriving malt industry.

As I was saddling my horse to leave, my brother Edmund turned up.

{*as Edmund*}   Will, I want to come back with you to London. I want to become an actor.

{*as Will*}   Ned, this is not a good time to do this. I know I have made a lot of money, but it's not like that for everyone. In fact, it's not like that for anyone. I went to London when you were thirteen years old. Things were different then. Right now, we haven't even got a theatre to play in. Look, ask me again next year and I'll see what I can do.

{*as Shakespeare*}   In the spring we presented Love's Labour's Won at the Curtain. Leaving the playhouse after the performance I walked straight into Ben Jonson!

{*as Jonson*}   What's the matter? Seen a ghost?

{*as Shakespeare*}   he said.

{*as Will*}   Yes. You. What happened? I never thought to see you again.

{*as Jonson*}   I'll tell you if you buy me a drink.

{*as Shakespeare*}   We went to the Flower Pot and found a table in the corner.

[Sits at table left.]

Ben set down his cup and lit his pipe.

{*as Jonson*}   Benefit of clergy.

{*as Shakespeare*} ...he said, with a self-satisfied smile.

{*as Will*}   What?

{*as Shakespeare*} ...I said.

{*as Jonson*}   Benefit of clergy. I read a neck verse.

{*as Will*}   Sorry, I don't understand.

{*as Jonson*}   Will, you never cease to amaze me. Your plays are
                     full of the most intricate understanding of legal
                     matters, yet you don't know what I mean when I
                     say I pled benefit of clergy. Sometimes I wonder
                     if you write those plays yourself at all. The law
                     states that a clergyman may not hang.

{*as Will*}   But you're not a clergyman.

{*as Jonson*}   The law says I am. The law sees no difference
                     between a clerk and a clergyman. A clerk is one
                     who can read and write Latin. I pled Benefit of
                     Clergy, they gave me a Latin verse to read out, I
                     did so... and saved my neck. I didn't save my
                     thumb, though.

{*as Shakespeare*} He held it out to me. It was branded "T" for
                     Tyburn. Next time he would hang.

[*Rises.*]

                     It was the coldest December any of us could
                     remember. The Thames froze over. The Lord
                     Chamberlain's Men had been looking forward to
                     this Christmas. We had a plan. When the
                     landowner left Shoreditch to celebrate Christmas
                     with his family, we moved house – literally. We
                     dismantled the Theatre and carried the timbers
                     across the river to our new site on the south bank.

We worked hard, day and night, sleeping in shifts, constantly concerned that the landlord would turn up and have us arrested for trespass. While children skated and revellers lit bonfires on the ice, we worked on, sliding the lighter timbers across the ice to save paying the toll for crossing London Bridge. In three days, it was done. When the landowner returned to Shoreditch all he found was an empty patch of ground. I wish I'd been there to see his face.

It was with a renewed optimism that we started the new century by presenting Henry V at the Curtain. The final link in the great series of history plays.

As we watched our new playhouse rising on our own ground, we started making plans for its opening. We discussed the type of play we would be performing there as opposed to our new indoor theatre at Blackfriars.

Burbage said...

{*as Burbage*}   One thing's for sure, we won't be dancing any jigs at Blackfriars. The stage is too small.

{*as Shakespeare*}   Kempe said,

{*as Kempe*}   That's all right. I can do my jigs solo.

{*as Shakespeare*}   Hemminges said...

{*as Hemminges*}   D-do we have to have j-jigs at all? Th-they really are so out of fashion.

{*as Shakespeare*}   Kempe rose to this.

{*as Kempe*}   Out of fashion? The audiences love them. They're
                    the only way to end a comedy, and after a tragedy,
                    they raise the spirits.

{*as Shakespeare*} Then Burbage put his foot right in it. He said to
                   Kempe...

{*as Burbage*}   Anyway, Kempe, you're over fifty now. Don't you
                    think you're a bit old to be dancing jigs?

{*as Shakespeare*} That did it. Kempe flew into a rage. All attempts
                   to calm him made him worse. Eventually, he
                   stormed out, saying...

{*as Kempe*}   You can keep your new playhouse, and your high-
                    and-mighty, too-good-for-jigs Blackfriars. I'm
                    leaving. But you haven't heard the last of me. I'll
                    show you who's too old for jigs!

[*Stops and turns.*]

                    We were left without a clown.

                    The new playhouse was a fine construction.

[*Moves about the stage, setting the scene.*]

                    The stage jutted out into the yard where the
                    groundlings stood, surrounding it on three sides.
                    They paid a penny. Those who sat undercover in
                    the three galleried tiers paid twopence. There
                    were threepenny seats as well, in the musicians'
                    gallery, overlooking the stage from behind, or
                    even sitting on the stage at either side. These
                    were for the sorts of people who came not so
                    much to see as to be seen.

                    Above the stage there were the heavens, copying

the device the Rose had installed for lowering an actor onto the stage for a spectacular effect.

With the heavens above and trapdoor below to lower us into hell, what could we call it but "The Globe"? All of life would be seen within this wooden O.

Flying high above the stage was a flag that could be seen for miles. It showed Hercules bearing the world on his shoulders with the legend: "Totus mundus agit histrionem" meaning – roughly, "All the world's a stage."

[He continues the quotation.]

And all the men and women merely players;
They have their exits and their entrances,
And one man in his time plays many parts...

[Sits on trunk.]

Suddenly Kempe's name was on everyone's lips. We hadn't heard of him since he stormed out of that meeting six months earlier. But now he was about to perform a spectacular feat. And he was taking bets on it. He was going to dance a jig all the way from London to Norwich! On 11th February 1600, amid much trumpeting and before an enormous crowd, he set off down the road to Norwich.

For the Globe's opening season, we performed Julius Caesar. And a new play by Ben Jonson, Every Man out of His Humour. This was a satire in which he caricatured several writers: Marston was portrayed as a verbose, turgid, pretentious man, with Thomas Dekker as his feeble companion. And I was in it as well. As a country bumpkin with a newly acquired coat of arms bearing the motto, "Not Without Mustard."

After three weeks Will Kempe arrived in Norwich. He had danced all the way. He had proved his point. He was not too old for jigs.

[Rises.]

And then came that unremarked miracle of the first night of Twelfth Night. On 3rd January 1601 the Florentine Duke Orsino arrived in England, at the secret invitation of the Queen, and only then was his visit made public and word sent to us that we should perform a play at Whitehall for the honoured guest. We had three days.

As if by magic, three days later we performed a play tailor-made for the occasion! Did the Queen question how we did it? No. Did anyone at court show any puzzlement whatever? No. They were all delighted with the play's relevance, with the knowing references, with the Twelfth Night theme, with the sparkling wit of the piece. But no one questioned how we had worked this miracle. The Queen received the praise lavished on her for our play most graciously.

But, no. It was no miracle, nor black magic, that brought the play from conception to full adult maturity in three days. It was prior knowledge. Christopher Marlowe was a part of Duke Orsino's entourage. He had been a member of his household staff for several years. And he had returned to England in the autumn, script in hand, well in advance of the Duke's party.

One other thing about Twelfth Night: Viola was played by a new young actor in the company, Edmund Shakespeare.

My father died. Ned and I returned to Stratford for the funeral. He had died happy, with the status of a gentleman that he had always wanted, and he had been fully accepted back into Stratford society. A short while before his death he had resumed his place on the town council. He had the comfort of knowing that he was not leaving a widow without support. We closed the shop and leased it out as an inn.

My father – methinks I see my father –

Where my lord?

In my mind's eye, Horatio.

Hamlet was back in the repertoire, but changed again – completely, magnificently changed. We had not performed it for six years, but in all that time in Italy, Marlowe had never left it alone. He had worked on it in his idle hours, following through ideas and thoughts that had been the currency of intellectual conversation in Florence until the character of Hamlet had become a model of a man for the new century.

What a piece of work is a man, how noble in reason, how infinite in faculties, in form and moving how express and admirable, in action how like an angel, in apprehension how like a god: the beauty of the world, the paragon of animals – and yet, to me, what is this quintessence of dust? Man delights not me – nor woman neither, though by your smiling you seem to say so.

Nor woman neither. I was visiting my wife in Stratford once or twice a year. This separation seemed to be a matter of no concern to Anne. And it was of no concern to me either. Anne and I had never had anything in common.

My journeys to and from Stratford had always been by way of Aylesbury and Banbury, but on the way back from my father's funeral, perhaps because I was feeling in low spirits and wished to delay my return to the problems of London and the Globe, I chose to go another route, by way of Woodstock and High Wycombe, calling at an inn in Oxford to book a bed for the night.

[Sits at table left.]

I sat in the bar and drank ale for an hour, observing the people coming and going. I was thinking of my father and the turns of fortune's wheel he had experienced during his life. And I was wondering about these people going about their daily business. I tried to read their faces. Were they happy or downhearted? Were they happily married? Were they faithful to their wives?

{as Jane}   I hope it's not my ale.

{as Shakespeare} said a voice.

[Looks up.]

It was the hostess of the inn.

{as Will}   Sorry?

{*as Shakespeare*} ...I said.

{*as Jane*}   I hope it's not my ale that's making you so unhappy.

{*as Will*}   Oh! No, thank you. It's very good.

{*as Jane*}   Then it must be something else.

{*as Shakespeare*} She sat down at my table.

{*as Jane*}   Want to tell me about it?

{*as Shakespeare*} We talked for two hours. I told her about my father's death. And then I told her about his life. And mine. She... listened. That's all. But as I talked to her I realized that this was what was missing in my life. Anne made no complaints about my absence in London. But she was not interested in what I was doing there. So long as I was bringing in money to run the house, that was all she wanted from me.

Jane Davenant showed me a warmth and understanding, and an interest. She listened while – with the aid of three-quarters of a gallon of ale – I talked. And, when I left the following morning to continue my journey to London, I was carrying yet another little secret.

[Rises.]

When Orsino returned to Italy, Marlowe remained behind. The Italian theme in the plays came to an end. The new Hamlet was the first in a series of remarkable plays. Now I was being looked upon as a genius – except by Ben Jonson, who looked upon me with increasing suspicion.

[Sits on trunk.]

In February the Globe put on a fencing match between two swordsmen, Turner and Dun. There was a terrible accident. Turner stabbed Dun in the eye. The blade went so far into the brain that he instantly died. The Globe was suddenly silent, stunned. I sat there reviewing the incident in my mind. This was an eerie acting out of a famous event – an invented event – an event that had never occurred. It was as if some force had decreed that this lie must become a truth – to preserve some balance in nature. I walked home feeling that our secret plot had conjured up this man's death.

Another death occurred the following month – one that was to shake the globe. The theatres were ordered to close as Queen Elizabeth lay dying. For five days the world held its breath, until on 24th March 1603, she finally left us. The reign of the Tudors, which had started one hundred and eighteen years earlier with the death of Richard III on Bosworth Field, came to an end. We were closed for two months.

[Rises and crosses left.]

I made another journey to Stratford, stopping at Jane Davenant's inn on the way, where I met... her husband. The merry widow I had assumed her to be was, in reality, a wife and mother. John Davenant was a quiet man, much respected in the town. He had at one time been the Mayor of Oxford. I slept alone that night.

But on my return journey to London, John was away.

[Sits left.]

Somehow the fact that she had a husband made me feel better about our affair. It was a shared guilt. And we shared something else as well.

{*as Will*}   Do you know, Jane? You are the only person I have entrusted with the truth about Marlowe. It is a burden that I have needed to share for a long time. Not with Walsingham, not even with Dick, but with someone else – someone who's not involved. Someone miles away from it. To the others, the leading player in this drama is Marlowe. It's all been about how Marlowe will survive, how he will cope with the deception, and so forth. When I'm with you, it's different. It's my story, not Kit's. It's about the effect it has had on me. This feeling that in helping Marlowe I am also robbing him. Both a thief and a benefactor. Nourishing that which I destroy. When I'm in London, just knowing that you, here, know about it, helps me to handle it.

[Rises and crosses to centre.]

{*as Shakespeare*}   When we re-opened the Globe, we had a new patron – King James. No longer the Lord Chamberlain's Men, we were the King's Men. Our first play was Sejanus. It was Ben Jonson's first tragedy. The audience hissed it off the stage. The plague deaths rose to over forty a week and we were closed again. We went on tour for the rest of the year.

The following summer, I found an opportunity to visit Jane in Oxford.

{*as Jane*}   William...

{*as Shakespeare*}   ...she said, clasping her husband's arm,

{*as Jane*}   Isn't it lovely? I'm going to have a baby.

{*as Shakespeare*}   Just from the way she said it, I knew that I was
                     the father. It was hours before I found a chance
                     to speak to her.

{*as Will*}   It's mine, isn't it?

{*as Shakespeare*}   I said.

{*as Jane*}   Yes, dear William. It is yours. And I will love it
                     the more for that. Don't worry. No one will know.
                     We're used to keeping secrets, aren't we?

{*as Shakespeare*}   During the night, the door of my room opened,
                     and she slipped into my bed beside me.

                     In the morning, her husband invited me to be the
                     child's godfather.

                     Burbage was at his peak as an actor. Edward
                     Alleyn had retired, leaving him with no rival
                     within sight. Burbage had painted a self-portrait,
                     which he hung in the Globe for the audience to
                     see as they came in. I asked him to paint mine.

*[Takes it out of trunk and proudly shows it to audience. He is disappointed
at the unenthusiastic reaction.]*

                     Well, it was a good likeness seven years ago. A lot
                     has happened to me since then.

                     I became godfather to my own son! William.

[Crosses and hangs picture on wall left.]

I saw my daughter Susannah married – to a doctor. And... I saw my brother Ned become a successful actor.

He played Cleopatra. He was all wily femininity. I swear that if we had actually had a woman up on that stage, she would not have had half the allure. With this performance, and his Lady Macbeth as well, he showed that he had a bright future.

One morning I found him sobbing in the corner by the stage.

[Crossing and crouching, right]

{*as Will*}   Ned, what is it? What's the matter?

{*as Edmund*}   It's my son. He's dead.

{*as Shakespeare*}   This made no sense to me.

{*as Will*}   Your son? You haven't got a son.

{*as Edmund*}   Yes, I have. I had. He's dead.

[Rises.]

{*as Shakespeare*}   A girl, who worked in the local brothels – kept by the Bishop of Winchester – had given birth to Ned's son two years earlier. Because of her profession as one of the so-called "Winchester geese" the whole affair had been kept totally secret.

We gave Edward, for that was the boy's name, a proper burial in a church two miles away. Just the three of us and the clergyman. Yet another secret.

At Christmas, we presented Antony and Cleopatra at Court, as well as The Devil's Charter. This was by Barnaby Barnes and it showed that the Pope was in league with the devil. The King liked that play very much.

Soon after, Ned took a fever and died. It wasn't the plague. We didn't know what it was. Looking back, I could see that he had been ill for some time, but I had put it down to grief at the loss of his son. And maybe it was.

Mother came down for the funeral. And my two brothers and my sister. And Anne and Judith, with Susanna and her new husband. Ned Shakespeare had become a well-respected actor over a very short period of time. We gave him a big send-off at St Saviour's Church in Southwark. All the actors in London seemed to be there. And, lurking unnoticed at the back of the church was Ned's girl, the Winchester goose. I found a moment to go to her and give her a few of Ned's things to remember him by. I went back to Stratford with mother and the others. I stayed there for most of the winter. I didn't tell mother about Ned's son.

In February I became a grandfather. They named her Elizabeth, after the late Queen.

My mother caught a cold and took to her bed. She was very frail at sixty-six years old. The cold became a fever. She had no strength to fight it off. I was at her bedside when she died.

A couple of visitors turned up in my orchard. Walsingham and Dick Field.

{*as Dick*}   It's about the sonnets, Will. We want to publish
                     them. They've been circulating among our small
                     group for so long, it's time the world had a chance
                     to read them.

{*as Will*}   But they give away the whole plot! We can't
                     publish them.

{*as Walsingham*}   My dearest friend has poured his heart into these
                     sonnets. If ever the truth about Marlowe is to be
                     told, these sonnets are the key.

{*as Will*}   But that is precisely why we cannot publish them!

{*as Dick*}   Supposing...

{*as Shakespeare*}   ...said Dick.

{*as Dick*}   Supposing we found a way of disguising the story
                     that they tell? After all, the beauty of these verses
                     isn't in their matter but in their manner, not in
                     the actual events to which they relate, but in the
                     poetry itself.

{*as Shakespeare*}   We spent two hours in the orchard, trying to work
                     out a way it could be done. We finally decided on
                     a plan. We took them into the house and spread
                     them out on the table. We spent the whole night
                     planning the sequence in which they were to be
                     published.

[*Downstage, working his way across, dealing with each sonnet sequence.*]

                     There were the seventeen sonnets for the Earl of
                     Southampton's   seventeenth   birthday,
                     commissioned in 1590 by Lord Burghley. These
                     were followed immediately by the earlier ones to
                     William Hatcliffe when he was given the mock

honour of Prince of Purpoole by the Gray's Inn law students. These two sequences ran into each other so smoothly that they disguised each other's subject matter. Then there were the sonnets to Luce Morgan, the dark-eyed courtesan Marlowe had loved and lost to Will Hatcliffe. In with these, we mixed those written to Walsingham before Marlowe's supposed death in Deptford. Planted in different places throughout the sequence, they misdirected the reader's attention, identifying themselves with the subject of the surrounding sonnets.

And we did the same with those written later from exile in Italy. By carefully placing them throughout the sequence, we disguised the true subject matter of this remarkable series of poems. We buried our secret deep, but, by ensuring that the exile sonnets, though separated, remained in their correct order, we left the key. At the heart of the sequence we placed the two sonnets which most identified the writer and his supposed death:

So then thou hast but lost the dregs of life,
The prey of worms, my body being dead,
The coward conquest of a wretch's knife,
Too base of thee to be remembered.

and…

[Slowly crossing to Marlowe's picture, right]

In me thou seest the glowing of such fire
That on the ashes of his youth doth lie,
As the death-bed, whereon it must expire,
Consum'd with that which it was nourish'd by.

"What nourishes me, consumes me."

Our secret was like a mine, buried deep enough, we hoped, that it would not be discovered in our lifetimes, to have us hoist with our own petard.

The Sonnets were published in 1609. They sold well.

I had little to do with the practical running of the King's Men now. And Marlowe had slowed to one play a year. The Globe continued to thrive. There were new, younger, writers producing good work. But none could come up with anything to rival Cymbeline, The Winter's Tale or The Tempest:

Our revels now are ended. These our actors,
As I foretold you, were all spirits, and
Are melted into air, into thin air;
And like the baseless fabric of this vision,
The cloud-capp'd towers, the gorgeous palaces,
The solemn temples, the great globe itself,
Yea, all which it inherit, shall dissolve;
And, like this insubstantial pageant faded,
Leave not a rack behind. We are such stuff
As dreams are made on, and our little life
Is rounded in a sleep.

The great Globe itself did dissolve. But not before it lost its guardian angel.

[Sits right.]

Marlowe died at Scadbury. I saw him before he died. He was with all his friends, members of the School of Night, Dick Field was there, and one or two others.

{*as Marlowe*} Will, I want to thank you for what you have done. You have enabled me to give my words life.

Without you, I would have carried on writing, but it would have been just paper gathering dust, maybe to be published one day as a curiosity, out of fashion. You and your actors have breathed my words into the ears of the world.

[Leaning forward.]

{*as Will*} Kit, it is I who should thank you. You have given my life a purpose. Without you, what would I have been? I would not have lasted long as an actor. I wasn't good enough. By being the means by which your magnificent plays have found life on the stage, my life has found a noble purpose. But that my name should be forever associated with these works and yours forever vilified...

{*as Marlowe*} What will be will be.

{*as Shakespeare*} said Kit.

{*as Marlowe*} And I have left clues. They are there in the plays for someone to find one day, just buried deep enough to protect you and Thomas and the rest of my good friends. I have left my signature. One day the truth will come out, you'll see.

{*as Will*} No, I won't.

{*as Shakespeare*} I said. He smiled.

{*as Marlowe*} No, you won't.

[Rises and crosses down centre.]

{*as Shakespeare*} Marlowe was dead. This, to the world, was old news. What could we do but in hugger-mugger to inter him in an unmarked grave in the grounds at

Scadbury?

Fear no more the heat o'th'sun
Nor the furious winter's rages
Thou thy worldly task hast done,
Home art gone, and ta'en thy wages.
Golden lads and girls all must,
As chimney-sweepers, come to dust.

He had left one last worldly task for me to do. All Is True was about Queen Elizabeth's father, Henry VIII. I copied it out the day we buried him. And I put it into Richard Burbage's hands the following morning.

The King's Men were now using Blackfriars as their main house. But I wanted All Is True to be performed at the Globe. It seemed right that it should be seen on the same stage as had held Hamlet, Macbeth, Othello and Lear. I supervised the production myself and played a minor role.

It did well. Until one afternoon, when we came to the moment of the King's surprise arrival at Cardinal Wolsey's banquet. The drum sounded, then the trumpet, the chambers were fired off... and a linstock, used for firing off the canon, touched the thatch in the roof.

We did what we could, but the fire spread rapidly. My first thought was for the playscripts. I managed to save most of them, but several were lost, Love's Labour's Won and Cardenio among them. Then I ran out to where the rest of the company were standing with their erstwhile audience. Condell and Hemminges had managed to salvage some scripts. Burbage was clutching his self-portrait. And we watched the great Globe

An Act of Will

itself dissolve before our eyes.

[Turns to audience.]

Now my charms are all o'erthrown,
And what strength I have's mine own,
Which is most faint.

[Gets another drink.]

I've been planning for this retirement. There's a
good income here. A few years ago, I bought a
hundred and twenty acres of land, which has
started paying for itself now. And I've got shares
in land in the surrounding countryside – four
hundred and forty pounds I paid. They're worth
a lot more now. I've made improvements to New
Place over the years. I bought a cottage in Chapel
Lane for my gardener. I've got two gardens, two
orchards. This is where I'll stay – with, perhaps,
the occasional visit to Oxford – in peaceful
retirement till I die.

Yes, I stopped over last night in Oxford with Jane.

[Massages back.]

Excuse me. That bed of hers is really
uncomfortable. I've got to do something about
that.

William is seven years old now.

[A sudden realization.]

I'll be spending a bit of time in Oxford from now
on. I've got too many beds here. I'm going to give
Jane my best bed.

And after my death? I've made plans for that, too.
Otherwise, they'll be putting me into a corner of
a Cathedral, with a representation of myself as
poet clutching a quill and a book. A place of
pilgrimage like a dead saint? No, Marlowe had a
right to all that. I'm not taking that from him.

I shall be buried here in Stratford. I have made
sure of it

[Picks up scroll of paper from table.]

The lease on these lands entitles me to be buried
in Holy Trinity church. And there my bones shall
stay. I have made sure of that, too, with this curse.

[Puts down scroll and picks up paper he was working on at beginning.]

Oh, believe me, no one will dare go against this.
I've been working on it all the way from Oxford,
trying to get the scansion right. I think I've got it
now.

Good friend for Jesus sake forbear
To dig the dust enclosed here.
Blest be the man that spares these stones
And curst be he that moves my bones.

Yes, I know, but it will have to do. A poor thing,
but mine own. Where's Marlowe when you need
him? He'd have given me an exit line – like
Prospero's...

Gentle breath of yours my sails
Must fill, or else my project falls,
Which was to please. Now I want
Spirits to enforce, art to enchant;
And my ending is despair
Unless I be reliev'd by prayer,

> Which pierces so, that it assaults
> Mercy itself, and frees all faults.
> As you from crimes would pardon'd be,
> Let your indulgence set me free.

> You will set me free?

[Again, a niggling worry about the audience. After all, who are they? And then a sudden, appalling thought occurs to him.]

> You're not... the Court? The Star Chamber?

[Suddenly frightened by what he has told them, he tries to laugh off his story.]

> It was only a story! A ridiculous story. A preposterous story. But it was a good one, no? If William Shakespeare can't tell you a good story, who can?

[Chuckles unconvincingly.]

> Mmm? What? Was it true? Oh! You wanted a true story? Is Romeo and Juliet true? Is Hamlet? What about Henry V? Henry VIII – or All Is...True? What is truth? Does everyone believing it make it true?

> In that case...

[Sits on trunk.]

[Rapidly.]

> I came to London in 1589 and I saw Marlowe's plays and I thought they were marvellous and I started writing. I discovered that I had a happy talent for it, which got better and better. I'd read a lot at school, Holinshead, Ovid, Plutarch. I was a studious lad, but I couldn't afford to go to university. I wrote the Henry VI plays first and Greene attacked me and Marlowe died in a fight in a tavern, it was very sad, and then I kept on

writing and acting for eighteen years and now I've stopped. Th-that's... the... truth.

Anyway... what does it matter?

[Rises and crosses to Marlowe's portrait.]

Look here upon this picture...

[Crosses to his own portrait.]

...and on this. Marlowe? Shakespeare?

What's in a name? That which we call a rose
By any other word would smell as sweet.

[Sits on trunk. Looks at audience. Looks from face to face. Then he throws back his head and laughs.]

Of course I wrote the plays!

[Still laughing.]

I wrote them.

[Gradually recovers.]

Me. I wrote them.

[Pause.]

I wrote them...

[A knowing smile.]

...didn't I?

[Blackout.]

AFTERWORD

One doesn't introduce a whodunnit by going over all the motivations that brought the murderer to commit the crime. So, when I was asked to write an introduction to *An Act of Will* for this edition, I thought I would have to leave out the twists in the story which form the "secret life" in the subtitle. These are secrets that should emerge as the play goes on.

But my interest in the likely existence of these secrets was what first led me to write the play. Therefore, what you are now reading is an afterword rather than an introduction.

So, if you have skipped to this page without first reading the play, go back right now!

As an actor with quite a bit of Shakespeare behind him, one day I realized that the only Shakespeare plays I really knew well were those I had been in. Others I had seen once or twice, maybe three times, but yet more were destined to remain a mystery to me unless I did something to rectify this. So, I started reading through his works in the sequence in which they are believed to have been written.

Then, I met the late Dolly Wraight. I had read one of her books, in which she made the claim that Christopher Marlowe had been the true author of one or two of Shakespeare's early plays. Subsequently, I had seen her interviewed in an episode of a TV series called *Bard on the Box*, putting forward the idea that Marlowe had written the whole lot, including the Sonnets and the other poems! I thought, dear me, this is very midsummer madness. But, meeting her, and talking to her, I was persuaded to buy her latest book, *The Story that the Sonnets Tell*.

I read it, and I was convinced. Admittedly, the matter is still open to dispute – and there continues to be a lot of that! There is evidence, but not enough to constitute proof. And my play is not an attempt to prove anything. It is, like any other play, based on a simple thought: if x happened, what might it be like? In my case: if Shakespeare did act as the voluntary front man for the continued output of a supposedly dead Marlowe, how would he feel about it? And, how does this idea fit in with the known facts?

My play doesn't fly in the face of known facts. No-one, so far, has challenged me on that score. This is the way it could have happened.

Known facts

It is a fact that a document declaring loyalty to the Catholic faith was found in the roof of Shakespeare's house. Also, Richard Field, publisher of Marlowe's work, had been raised in Stratford and was more likely than not to have known Shakespeare during his youth. The discrepancy in the records, involving William and the two Annes, does exist. Sir Thomas Lucy (well-known for the, possibly apocryphal, deer-shooting incident) was appointed to hunt down Catholic priests. The thousand pounds which, according to one story, came suddenly into the possession of Shakespeare, supposedly did so at roughly the time of Marlowe's "death". The apparent coincidence of name between Hamnet and Hamlet is purely that. It was customary to name children after their Godparents.

Facts open to interpretation

Now, to the more controversial assertions. Robert Greene's *Groatsworth of Wit*, containing the much-quoted single paragraph with the alleged attack on Shakespeare, has been cited over and over again as evidence that Shakespeare was not only in London at the time, but was so well-known as a playwright as to be easily identified by an oblique reference to him as a "Shake-scene". But it is only to modern eyes that this looks like evidence. It is the capital "S" that does this. Greene uses "Shake-scene" merely as a pejorative term for an actor. The Elizabethan printer followed normal practice in capitalising this common noun, as he did the words "Crow", "Tygers" and "Players" in the very same sentence. If he had intended it to refer to a name he would have italicised it, as he does "Johannes fac totum".

The man who best fits this Jack-of-all-trades description is Edward Alleyn. As Wraight puts it, in *The Story that the Sonnets Tell*, Alleyn "… was the greatest actor of his day, at the age of twenty-six… a fine musician, a successful theatre-manager, a property owner and landlord, a banker and money-lender, and (most galling to Greene) a successful, if minor playwright…" He is known to have written *Tambercam*, and there is no reason to believe that the other nine plays he sold were not also written by him. All the evidence points to Alleyn as being this "Shake-scene" actor. The "tiger's heart" reference being easily identified as a parody of a line in *Henry VI Part 3* would seem to nail the matter in favour of Shakespeare, were it not for the fact that the play only appears in print with that title for the first time in the First Folio of 1623, seven years after Shakespeare's death. The play had been first presented on stage under the title *The True Tragedy of Richard Duke of York*, by an unnamed author, shortly before Greene wrote this attack. And who had played York? None other than the actor-manager who employed Greene, Edward Alleyn. Since this one reference constitutes the only hint that Shakespeare was an established playwright at the time, the "evidence" disappears in a puff of smoke. And the author of *The True Tragedy* could well have been Marlowe.

Twelfth Night

And then there's the little matter of *Twelfth Night*. John Manningham, a law student at Middle Temple, saw a performance of *Twelfth Night* at the beginning of February 1602. But, from the wording of Manningham's diary entry, it is unlikely that this was the first performance of the play. There certainly was a play performed on Twelfth Night that year, and it was presented in front of Queen Elizabeth and Don Virginio Orsino, Duke of Bracciano. But every Shakespeare pundit dismisses the possibility of this play being *Twelfth Night*. For instance, my copy of the Arden edition (ed. JM Lothian and TW Craik) asserts, "… it is most unlikely that Shakespeare could have composed it and the actors rehearsed it between 25 December 1600 (when the date of Orsino's visit became known) and 6 January 1601..." Well, true, it is unlikely that Shakespeare could have achieved that. So, it is certainly evidence of... something. And my play presents a scenario of what that something might have been.

"Much virtue in If."

Now, some unavoidable ifs, that Touchstone would have been proud of. If Marlowe's death was faked to avoid his torture and execution, and it happened roughly as outlined in the play – and then he continued to write – what would he have written? The *Sonnets*, as analysed and sorted into categories by AD Wraight, tell the story of exile in Italy. And, between Marlowe's supposed death and the turn of the century, apart from the history plays, all of the plays have an Italian setting. So (continuing this line of thought), does this indicate that, after the presentation of *Twelfth Night*, Marlowe found himself back in England? Thomas Thorpe, who wrote the cryptic dedication for the published *Sonnets*, seems to hint (in a letter to Edward Blount, the publisher of Marlowe's *Hero and Leander*) that he's spotted Marlowe in St Paul's churchyard on several occasions. This is in the autumn of 1600, so some months before Orsino's visit. in any case, from this point on, the exclusively Italian theme of the plays comes to an end.

Another "if": supposing Shakespeare had been receiving manuscripts from Marlowe in Italy, and then presenting them as his own to the company at the Globe, would he not have been at pains to disguise the true authorship? And, would that not have entailed copying them out in his own hand? Handwriting was as easily identifiable then as now. "Alas, Malvolio, this is not my writing,/Though I confess much like the character:/ But, out of question, 'tis Maria's hand..." (Olivia, *Twelfth Night*, Act V, Scene one.) If Shakespeare had received Marlowe's "foul papers" (i.e. the initial manuscript, corrections and crossings out and all), copied them out, and presented his copy of a new play to his company, would that pristine copy not be worthy of comment? Of course, and here it is, from Ben Jonson: "I remember the players have often mentioned it as an honour to Shakespeare, that in his writing

(*whatsoever he penned*) he *never* blotted out a line." [My italics.]
And, here are two of those players: "... we have scarce received
from him a blot in his papers." This from Heminges and Condell,
compilers of the First Folio. This is often overlooked, but I think it
is well worth mentioning. (And so, it seems, did his fellow actors.)
John Mitchell, in *Who Wrote Shakespeare?* (Thames and Hudson),
confuses the issue by applying these remarks, not to the new scripts
as used by the actors for the first productions, but to the later, old,
used copies and printed quarto scripts used by Heminges and
Condell in compiling the First Folio – concluding as a result that
this is "an editorial fiction."

A couple of other pieces of speculation that I have adopted and
used in the play: it has been argued that the Chandos portrait in
the National Portrait Gallery in London was actually painted by
Richard Burbage; also, the writer William Davenant claimed, at
various times, to have been Shakespeare's son... and godson. He
could easily have been both. As I have said, it was the practice to
name children after their godparents.

What's in a (pub's) name?

When I was a small child, I used to enjoy *Bill and Ben, the Flower
Pot Men* on the television. So, when I was writing this play, and it
came to choosing a name for the tavern in which William (Bill)
Shakespeare and Ben Jonson meet for a chat, it amused me to call
it "The Flower Pot". The meeting takes place after a performance
at The Curtain. Some years after writing *An Act of Will*, I read *Mr
Minns & His Cousin*, the short story which was Charles Dickens'
very first piece of writing. It contains the line, "'Now mind the
direction," said Budden; "the coach goes from the Flowerpot, in
Bishopsgate-street, every half hour.'" A footnote in my edition
added that the Flowerpot was a "well-known inn in Bishopsgate,
City of London, from which short-stagecoaches started." It adds
that the inn was demolished in 1866. I had invented the name
purely as a joke for my own amusement! I have not checked, but if,
268 years earlier, in 1598, this coaching inn was already in
existence, just around the corner from The Curtain, my choice of

name is pretty startling. In fact, if it were played upon a stage now, I should condemn it as an improbable fiction.

– Michael McEvoy
2019

An introduction to a monologue, as Shakespeare, suggested for use as an audition piece

This piece is pretty self-explanatory. William Shakespeare is telling his story to us. And, he's reliving it.

He relives the bewilderment he felt as a young lad witnessing his father seeming to fall apart, and not understanding why. (The reason, that eventually emerges, is that, as a Catholic and a local council member, John Shakespeare is feeling under increasing pressure as distrust of Catholics gains a hold.)

And Will relives the joy he experienced when Anne Whateley agrees to marry him – followed by the weight of responsibility that gradually descends onto his shoulders as the prospect of this marriage slips through his fingers, and he finds himself married to the wrong Anne.

– MM

{*as Shakespeare*} I was eighteen years old. It was the summer of 1582. And I was in love with Anne Whately. Father got involved in a drunken brawl and was told to attend the court to apologize and guarantee to keep the peace in future. He refused. He was fined forty pounds. Things were going wrong for our family and I didn't understand why.

And then it happened. I lost my virginity. And with it my youth. And with it my freedom. Anne Hathaway of Shottery was eight years older than me. An experienced woman. She knew what she was doing. Oh, don't misunderstand. I was no unwilling participant. But this was more than a roll in the hay to her. As I said, she knew precisely what she was doing.

And I sensed this immediately. I felt I was in danger of losing something precious. Seized with a sense of urgency, I went straight over to Temple Grafton and asked Anne Whateley to marry me. And she said yes! It was the beginning of October. December 2nd to January 2nd is Advent, during which there can be no marriages. I had to move swiftly, but within a few weeks we were given the necessary parental approval. And, on November 27th, we were issued with a marriage licence.

With the licence in my hand, at last I could relax. I told my friends immediately, of course. And she told her friends. And my parents told theirs. And her parents told theirs. And that night two men from Shottery came knocking at our door.

Nature had taken her course and Anne Hathaway's insurance policy against a spinster's old age had paid its dividend.

The following morning, I was signing the register again, accompanied by these two gentlemen – who stood surety that I would go ahead with my marriage to Anne Hathaway.

Forty pounds to indemnify the bishop, should Anne Whately assert her prior claim. They needn't have worried. When her parents found out that I had got Anne Hathaway with child, they were happy that their daughter had escaped the clutches of such a ne'er-do-well. And so, I was married… *[Checks that he is not being overheard.]* …to the wrong Anne. Did I tell you she was eight years older than me? Well… She still is.

"…Let still the woman take

An elder than herself. So wears she to him.
So sways she level in her husband's heart."

So... she moved into our house. And six months
later Susanna was born. Suddenly I was an adult,
with responsibilities.

**An introduction to a second monologue, as both Shakespeare and
Will, similarly suggested for use as an audition piece**

*This is almost as self-explanatory as the other monologue. It is also a bit
shorter. Again, the older Shakespeare is telling us his story, but this time,
in reliving it, he actually slips into the situation where the younger Will is
expressing to Jane Davenant his feelings about yet another burden of
responsibility: his deception, not of Jane's husband, but of the world.*

*He is a conspirator (with Thomas Walsingham, Richard Field and
Christopher Marlowe, who is presumed dead) to act as front man for
Marlowe's continued output of plays. And the relief of being able to relax
his guard, and talk openly about it with Jane, is immense.*

– MM

{*as Shakespeare*} I made another journey to Stratford, stopping at
Jane Davenant's inn on the way, where I met...
her husband. The merry widow I had assumed her
to be was in reality a wife and mother. John
Davenant was a quiet man, much respected in the
town. He had at one time been the Mayor of
Oxford. I slept alone that night.

But on my return journey to London, John was
away.

[Sits.]

Somehow the fact that she had a husband made me feel better about our affair. It was a shared guilt. And we shared something else as well.

{*as Will*}   Do you know, Jane? You are the only person I have entrusted with the truth about Marlowe. It is a burden that I have needed to share for a long time. Not with Walsingham, not even with Dick, but with someone else – someone who's not involved. Someone miles away from it. To the others, the leading player in this drama is Marlowe. It's all been about how Marlowe will survive, how he will cope with the deception, and so forth. When I'm with you, it's different. It's my story, not Kit's. It's about the effect it has had on me. This feeling that in helping Marlowe I am also robbing him. Both a thief and a benefactor. Nourishing that which I destroy. When I'm in London, just knowing that you, here, know about it, helps me to handle it.

Also published by 49Knights

EDINBURGH49

REVIEWING BEYOND THE FRINGE

The review team at *Edinburgh49* scours the listings, checking out the best and the brightest from Edinburgh's flourishing creative scene, signposting the top places to score your arts fix.

Start with 52 weeks in the year, take away three, and you have *Edinburgh49*. We provide year-round reviews and arts stories from across Scotland's capital. *Edinburgh49 +3* is our dedicated summer festivals coverage, giving us a chance to support friends old and new with lively and insightful content.

This script is published by 49Knights

49KNIGHTS
ABOUT US

49Knights was established to do for play scripts what the fair trade movement has done for tea and coffee - to reduce the distance between the producer and the consumer so as to bring maximum reward to the producer and and maximum quality to the consumer. The artists we collaborate with retain 100% ownership of their work and the performance rights. Getting published with 49Knights empowers writers to reach new audiences both in print and on stage.

Our approach to content is inspired by Ben Jonson's 1616 Folio. Jonson was the first English playwright to edit his plays to be read as well as performed. We hope that the result is as immersive an experience as seeing the scripts performed live. As publishers, our job is to be the studio sound engineer, getting the artist on record with a minimum of distortion and distraction. It's vital to the integrity of each project that the artist makes all the artistic decisions - it's their voice that matters.

BROWSE OUR TITLES